With a master's degree in Clinical Psychology, P. Angel Marie Rogers is a certified Clinical Hypnotherapist and Life Coach. Her primary purpose in life is to help people fall in love with themselves and life by overcoming obstacles that hinder self-love, success, and peace. Motivated by one of her clients, she started writing books as a way to accomplish her goal to help others.

On March 21, 2019, my grandmother wrote me a letter that read: My dearest Patricia, I am so proud of you. You can open your book, Fuck Fear, to any page, any day, and find enlightenment. Even for your 80-year-old grandmother.

– Love Always, Amelia L. Williams

The words in that letter meant so much to me. I dedicate this book to my loving grandmother. I love you forever and always!

This book is also dedicated to Babylove, my mother. I can't even think of what I should say on this page for a dedication to you because I want to say so much. Therefore, I will simply say I love you and know that is more than enough for you. I love you forever and always!

P. Angel Marie Rogers

F**k Fear

AUSTIN MACAULEY PUBLISHERS™

LONDON • CAMBRIDGE • NEW YORK • SHARJAH

Ordering Information
Quantity sales: Special discounts are available on quantity purchases by corporations, associations, and others. For details, contact the publisher at the address below.

Publisher's Cataloging-in-Publication data
Rogers, P. Angel Marie
F**k Fear

ISBN 9781645755609 (Paperback)
ISBN 9781645755616 (Hardback)
ISBN 9781645755623 (ePub e-book)

Library of Congress Control Number: 2021901985

www.austinmacauley.com/us

First Published (2021)
Austin Macauley Publishers LLC
40 Wall Street, 33rd Floor, Suite 3302
New York, NY 10005
USA

mail-usa@austinmacauley.com
+1 (646) 5125767

First and foremost, I have to acknowledge God, who has loved me, guided me, and blessed me time after time.

My husband, Walid, for showing me that unconditional love exists in the human flesh. I love you.

Last, but certainly not least, my daughter, Honor. You, little girl, have motivated me beyond measure. At this point in life, you can't even talk, but you have taught me so much.

I literally could not fit everyone I wanted to thank. There are so many members of my family and friends that gave me words of encouragement and motivated me throughout my life, writing experiences, career, and so on. Thank you all! You all know who you are, if you have to question it, then it's not you.

Table of Contents

Meditations and questions for people that want to achieve their desires despite having fears.

How to Put This Book to Use

If only you can accept the truth, without questioning it, that you are powerful, unstoppable, creative, loved, intelligent, amazing, worthy, wonderful, important, excellent, beautiful, blessed, valuable, special, and so much more, you would be all of those things.

That is the purpose of this book! To guide you to feel, believe, know, and think that you are the shit because you are! This book was written to help you get rid of self-doubt and fill your being with certainty. Most importantly, this book was written to help you put fear aside and fall in love with yourself and life.

This book is not meant to be read from cover to cover and then thrown someplace where you can't find it. Use the book! I suggest that you look through the contents and focus on the topics that will be of value to you. If you are a person that likes to read from cover to cover, then so be it. That is just perfect for you. If the advice resonates with you, meditate on it, talk about it, and use it. If you don't agree with what you read, then fuck you. Just kidding. If you don't agree just simply disregard it and find another section. If you don't agree with anything in the book, disregard the entire book and find another book that feels good to you. Everything is not for everyone.

You don't have to read in any specific order. Regardless of how you decide to read it, take your time. Read a section and then pause and reflect. Answer the questions. Pause and reflect. Then do the meditation. It takes time to create a habit, so I recommend spending at least 21–30 days on one meditation. Set the start and end date in your phone or on your calendar, and set an alarm every day to do the meditation.

There are some checkboxes starting on page 152 to help you stay organized with the meditations. I have also recorded the meditations so you can listen to them on Vimeo which you can find on my channel at vimeo.com/angelmarie. Listening to the meditations, instead of reading them, may be easier and more beneficial for auditory people.

If doing a daily meditation sounds like too much for you, then don't do it. But you must do something different to see a change in your life. It doesn't have to be the meditations, but you have to try something new. If you don't try something new, even a blind person can see that you will probably be the same person you have always been and you will be doing the same thing you have always been doing and you will feel the same way you have been feeling and you will think the same way you have been thinking and you will settle for the same thing you have been settling for and you will still be talking about the same thing you have been talking about. Just pay attention to how your habits have been working out for you this far. Just a heads up, if you want to keep your same habits, you are going to keep the life you have now. Nothing is going to change for you if you don't change. You have to do something different to see something different PERIOD.

To lose weight, you have to work out or get surgery, either way, it's doing something different. To learn multiplication, you have to write or say them over and over again. To learn how to play the piano, you practice over and over again. You have to put in the work for everything in life, which includes letting go of fear and attaining your desires. What I am recommending is light work. It will take no more time than a half-hour TV show, it can be done on the train, on the toilet, in the tub, before bed. Just try it!

If listening to meditations are not for you, then find something for you that will work. Remember everything is not for everyone. Whatever you do, just know that in order to yield new results in your life, you have to do something different than what you have been doing this far. Meditations are not the end all be all, but they are one source to place positive messages inside of you that may eventually come real in your life. The point is that there is no harm in trying. So, try your best to give the meditations a try!

Introduction

"They Say" you can't judge a book by its cover. I say you can't just believe everything "They Say" because the things "They Say" may not apply to you or your situation. In some cases, you can judge a book by its cover and be right. In other cases, you can judge a book by its cover and be wrong. You have to have discernment and follow your instincts to come to your own conclusions. Don't readily and easily accept everything "They Say." "They Say" a lot of things! By the way, who are "They?" I define the They Sayers as people who say that things are true for everybody just because it was true in their personal situations. We will get into depth about the "They Sayers" later in the book. Anyway, in this case, "They" are wrong. You can judge this book by its cover. This book is all about telling fear, and any feeling related to it, to fuck off. I know the title is very vulgar. But in my defense, the vulgar title isn't half as bad as living a life full of fear that will rob you from having a peace of mind. Fear will stop you from pursuing your dreams. Fear can keep you away from true love. So, I made the title the way it is to emphasize the feeling I have about fear. On top of emphasizing the feeling I have, I honestly don't give a fuck about what anyone has to say regarding the message that was placed on my heart. I'm not saying fuck you, so don't get hung up on the word fuck or any other profane words you may come across (a heads up). As long as a person is not using his or her words to tear down another person, who cares what words are used. If you are a person that cares, I don't want to sound insensitive to your feelings, but we are tackling bigger problems, FEAR, not curse words.

Moving right along, this book also provides some meditations, hence the meditation pose on the cover. The meditations will help you get rid of fear IF you affirm the words, and then DON'T say, do, or be anything that contradicts the words you affirm. You have to keep your attention, energy, and focus only on what you want and never on what you do not want. Reading this book will help you understand why it is important to focus solely on what you want and disregard anything contrary to it and this book will give suggestions on how to do that.

Your dominant belief, whether it be fear or faith, will manifest in your life. Your beliefs are stored in your subconscious mind which makes your subconscious mind your partner for a successful life. Most people are aware that they have a subconscious mind, but many people don't know exactly what it does. The goal of the subconscious mind is to attract circumstances and situations in your reality that match the beliefs you have within. Think of it as soil that will grow any seed you plant in it. Your habitual thoughts, beliefs, and actions are seeds that are constantly being sown/planted.

Since you reap what you sow, you cannot manifest health, wealth, and positivity by planting unhealthy, poor, and negative thoughts in your mind. Just like there is an inability to grow an apple tree from a peach seed, you are unable to grow positivity from negativity. This is law! The subconscious mind does not judge or discriminate what you plant in its soil. It will manifest success and health just as easily as it manifests failure and sickness. It will manifest a hundred-dollar bill just as easily as it manifests a penny. It will manifest happiness just as quickly as it manifests sadness. The subconscious mind does not evaluate things like your conscious mind does, so YOU have to be conscious of what you plant in the garden of your mind. It's your job to weed out the toxic messages, programs, and beliefs. You are the garden keeper of your mind.

Every time you learn something new, you grow new brain cells. Which is good news because that means your brain can be rewired with new information. New beliefs will yield different circumstances in your life because your beliefs are correlated with your actions. Your beliefs determine the thoughts you have. The thoughts you have determine your feelings. Your feelings determine how you act and react. Because of this cycle, in order to manifest new or different things in your life, you have to think, believe, and do differently than what you do now. You attract what you believe. You attract what you put out. You attract what you vibrate. You can take a look at your life, as it is right now, to see what you have been vibrating or what you have been believing about yourself. If you are lacking something, do you feel worthy to have what you are lacking? If you are constantly physically sick, are you mentally or emotionally unhealthy, worrying, and depressed? If you want something in your life to be different, you have to DO and BE something different. Take the time to reflect on what changes you would like to see in your life and then take the time to see how you feel about your ability to accomplish those changes.

This book is written for all those people holding themselves back from doing something that they always wanted to do. For those holding themselves back from being who they want to be. For those people not holding themselves accountable for not having what they want. For those allowing their power to be outside of themselves by claiming this person "caused me" to miss out on this, or that person "made me" the way I am. Blaming the "lack of" on everything and everyone outside of self. Lack of money, lack of a significant other, lack of a good job, lack of a dream house, and so on. In some cases, blaming seems justified. I am wise enough to know that there are systems that exist that cause oppression, violence, low self-esteem, and poverty. I worked enough to know that some children go through many different traumatic stressors that cause neurological damage which in turn creates depression, lack of impulse of control and substance dependencies when they become adults. I know that there are direct pipelines from poor education systems to prison systems. I lived long enough to experience systems that perpetuate inequality.

In case the cover did not give it away, I am a black woman. Moreover, I am a dark-skinned black woman. I have experienced many isms: racism, colorism, and sexism. I am aware that all men and women are not truly born equally because of these isms. I said all of that to say that I understand adversities exists in this world. I have sympathy, empathy, and compassion for the many people that are facing these realities because they exist. Whatever maladaptive behaviors that you developed to escape your adversity was valid at the time you were forced to develop them. Whether it is drinking, smoking, or not trusting others, for example, I understand that they were developed as a protectant factor and may now be your automatic responses. I understand that they are not the actual problem that you have or had, they were merely a way for you to find a solution to your problems. But let me reassure you, there is another solution that will bring you comfort!

When it is all said and done, I remember that we are all from the same source. We may not all come from the same family line, but we all came from the same spirit. I personally believe in God, so when I talk about this higher power, spirit, and source, God is my reference. I understand that there may be some people that get a hold of this book that do not believe in God. Don't stop now, you can enjoy this book without feeling subjected to my spiritual belief system. Be okay with everyone not being the same and then life will become a little sweeter. Anyway, I believe that we all have the same power within us. Although life circumstances can move us away from FEELING that power, it is still there. Some circumstances can truly make us feel like we don't have any power at all. BUT the power is there because no one or nothing can take that away from you. Tap into it and stay aligned with it because that source can get you through any circumstance that feels fucked up.

Don't bow down and accept anything that is unacceptable. Don't accept anything unacceptable from YOURSELF or anyone else. Just remember you can't fight a good fight if powerlessness is running your system. In

21

other words, if you feel defeated you will be defeated. If you feel powerless, you will not have power. If you feel held down, you will stay down. Get up! Let those negative things motivate you to do and be something positive! Before you fight to get rid of those systems and circumstances that exist in this world, fight for yourself. What good would you be to anyone else if you show up bitter, negative, down, and defeated? What can you do in this moment with the resources that you have now? Call a counselor, get law enforcement behind you, leave a situation, speak up, enroll in a program, reach out to someone, what can you do? The answer is never nothing. Work on yourself! Empower yourself! You are only as strong as your weakness! There is a power within you that is bigger, stronger, and badder than any adversity that exists. It will help you get through what you deem as a hopeless. Tap into that power. Go within and come out ready to face life's challenges.

Challenges have always existed, and they will continue to exist for a long time. I personally want everyone to overcome challenges. I want everyone to feel loved and spread love. I want everyone to be able to eat when they are hungry, to walk outside and feel safe, to be at home and feel protected. Ultimately, I want everyone to be so happy that they do not want to cause pain on somebody else. I know that I am no good at helping others when I feel helpless within myself. I know that if I see a problem and act like the people that are the problem, that will make me a part of the problem. It's so easy to hate someone when you feel like he or she deserves hate. Those feelings will only get you so far. Being mad, stressed, and worried has never stopped negativity from happening. You know what has? Energy towards solutions. Actions towards solutions. Your energy shouldn't be focused on the things you hate because the things you hate will win thanks to you and all of the other people feeding it more energy. Which side are you going to be on when you face the challenges? The overwhelmed, bogged down, fearful side that feeds negativity? Or the hopeful, mighty, and faithful said that feeds positivity. Your energy NEEDS to go toward the things you would love to see manifested. That choice, no matter how it seems, is up to you. Let your circumstances help you decide what you want. Let your focus stay on the outcome you want to see!

This book is a program of motivation and inspiration to help you work through fear and release limitations. After each section, there will be some questions that I encourage you to answer and I encourage you to answer them honestly. Try not to zoom through the questions. I added questions because they can be a powerful motivator. Questions make you think, reflect, and direct your focus. They can spark change in your life. A question is the first step to solve a problem. Furthermore, questions make you cross-examine the world around you and your world within you. It's time to awaken that inner three-year-old child that used to ask a ton of questions, with the question, "but why?" being the main one so you can review the present reality that everyone readily accepts.

After the questions, there is a meditation related to each topic discussed. Read it several times, meditate on the words, realize the meaning, and mentally affirm it. Affirm to be what you desire to be, do, or have and focus only on that. There is no need to focus on the opposite. You have to say and do nothing that contradicts your affirmation as you wait on the fulfillment of what you affirmed. God made things out of himself simply by speaking and he gave us the ability to do the same by using his power within us. Our word is law, so affirm what you want and then KNOW that you have manifested it. Everyone is able to manifest everything they desire, but everyone doesn't take advantage of that capability because everyone doesn't know how to do it. One way is to control your subconscious mind. Most people allow their subconscious mind to control them. People say they are going to be something and then a doubtful thought pops up and then they start second-guessing themselves. That second-guessing will hold you back. If you are not living the life you want, you need to change your beliefs. In order to change your belief, you have to override what is already implanted in your mind, and the meditations will help with that.

The purpose of the meditations is to align with God. It is not for the purpose of influencing God to change because "he has not treated you fairly." It is not for the purpose of trying to convince God to change your life for you. It is up to you to change your life by changing the way you think, feel, and behave. The change in your life will be based on your belief. God is the same God as yesterday, a decade ago, a thousand years ago, and will be the same in the future. God is love and love is within you. God is good and all good is available to you. You have to bring yourself to the point that you believe you can have all the great things. Align with peace, harmony, and abundance. Repetition is key to believing, so I suggest that you meditate daily. You have to put the work in to change any fearful beliefs in your subconscious mind that's holding you back.

Section 1: Fear

"Fear is not real. The only place that fear can exist is in our thoughts of the future. It is a product of our imagination, causing us to fear things that do not, at present, and may not ever exist. That is near insanity. Do not misunderstand me danger is very real, but fear is a choice."

– Will Smith

Fuck Fear

Most times, fear is the reason people **focus** on things they don't want. Fear is also the reason people **settle** for things they don't want because fear plays a part in making people **disbelieve** in themselves. Fear has the potential ability to hold you back from your dreams for as long as you live. Fear is something that uninvitedly shows up in our lives. It is pretty much unavoidable, but it's ignorable. Fear is that little voice that pops in our heads when we are making important decisions, thinking about our dreams, or when we are looking in the mirror. You do not have to believe that voice. Disregard it!

If we believe the voice, it can steal our peace within by making us feel nervous, unworthy, unwanted, upset, and incompetent. It can cause stress or illness, and it can bring down the level of our self-love and esteem. Fear can be very subtle, so most people don't realize that they fall victim to fear's influence. It's something that will have us fucked up, if we give in to it, so fuck fear. Fuck what fear is talking about. Fuck listening to it. Fuck believing it.

Change the topic of fear. Meditate fear away. Do the opposite of what fear says.

We need to treat fear like anything else we don't believe in life. Fear belongs in the category with Santa, the Tooth Fairy, and the monster under the bed. If you got a letter in the mail that says, "You suck!" and it's addressed from Santa's elves, you will laugh. You won't dwell on the fact that it said you suck and start questioning if the message has meaning. My point is don't dwell on what fear says. It's a fairytale merely because it is a made-up story in your head.

Even if your fear is based on an event in your past, it's still a choice to fear. Your past event may never happen again. More importantly, the past no longer exists, therefore your current situation or future situations have nothing to do with the past UNLESS you CHOOSE to make them related. Choose wisely: disregard fear. If fear says, "you're going to fail, don't try it," try it anyway and if you don't succeed the first time, try again because there is no such thing as failing or losing. You either win, or you learn! I was astonished to learn that play-doh, originally was created to be a wallpaper cleaner, but failed. Now it's a multi-million-dollar product that is a favorite to most kids. Speaking of wallpaper, bubble wrap started off as wallpaper, but failed. Now bubble wrap is a billion-dollar product. The moral of the stories is to just do what you love. Do what inspires you. Just create and let the CREATOR handle what happens with the end product.

To stay on a positive note, I want to make it clear that I don't view fear as negativity anymore. I started viewing it as a great motivator. We have to change our perspective on it in order to gain good from it. What you resist persists, so don't resist fear. Assist fear to change into faith. When fear pops up and says you will fail, simply say *naw, fear, let me tell you the outcome God promised me.* When fear pops up and says there ain't enough for you, say *wait, fear, God said there is abundance.* When fear says you can get sick, say, *fear, let me remind you that I was made in pure spirit and spirit can neither hurt nor be harmed, I will remain healthy because I am made in the image of the almighty.* Thanks, fear, for the reminder of who I am and what I am capable of doing! Look at fear as something that is checking in on your faith.

In a lot of cases, a person doesn't go after his desire because his FEAR is outweighing FAITH. You don't start something because you fear it's not the right time. You don't finish something because you fear it's not going to be perfect. You don't say something because you fear others will not like it. You don't get into something because you fear you may get the same disappointing results as before. You don't invest because you fear you will lose money. You don't do something because you fear someone else is doing it better. You don't go somewhere because you fear you may get sick. You don't ask for something because you fear being told no. You don't try a business because you fear you may fail.

Well, you are completely, absolutely, totally, 100% right. Any fear you BELIEVE is true, becomes true when it pertains to YOU. Think about it, not everyone fails at that very thing you want to do. So why would you fail? The answer is simple; you FEARED you would fail. Synonymously, you BELIEVED you would fail! What you fear will come upon you. It may not be what you feared specifically, but your fear will manifest something in your life that you dislike. The more you fear, the more life will give you something to fear over. If you focus on something that isn't working, it doesn't work even more. If you focus on pain, life will give you something else to feel pain over. If you focus on not having enough, life will give you more of not enough.

Anxiety of flying or driving – fear. Not quitting a job that you hate because you're scared you may not get another one – fear. Not leaving a spouse that is abusive because you may not find love again – fear. Thinking you will never have a baby because you tried for years to conceive – fear. Thinking your parents will be disappointed in you because it took you six years to graduate versus four years – fear. In a lot of cases, people live in fear because something happened to someone else. Never even experienced it themselves, but afraid because of what may happen because it happened to someone else. Fear disappears when you act in spite of it. The good thing about fear is that it is just a feeling that comes from a thought. That means you can master your fears by concentrating on a different thought. They are lifeless thoughts until you breathe life into them by putting energy into them. It is your choice whether you give power to them. To reach the goal of eliminating fear, we have to choose the right thoughts and keep on choosing them. In turn, we keep choosing to feel good and by feeling good we can take good actions.

You better let fear go because what you fear will come upon you. It may not even be specific to the thing you fear, but if you are open to ANYTHING negative you are open to EVERYTHING negative. You may fear germs because you may get sick. The universe doesn't hold back on sickness. If you fear that you will get the flu, you are putting stress on your body and on your immune system which will leave you open to getting the flu, HIV, a headache, a bellyache, a hangnail, and so on. If you fear driving because you may get into an accident, you can be walking and a tree falls on you because the universe will give you an accident. Let me make this clear now, I am not saying illnesses and diseases come from fear, I am saying that you put yourself at risk and you are more susceptible to illnesses and diseases when you fear, have anxiety, worry, and so on. It's just like cigarettes don't cause cancer for everyone that smokes, but everyone that smokes it is at risk for cancer because the toxins put your body through stress. Negative feelings are toxic and they do cause chemical reaction in your body.

YOU GET WHAT YOU PUT OUT. Karma doesn't just apply to the person who donated a million dollars to a shelter. Karma doesn't just apply to a killer. Karma applies to every little thing and every big thing, and everything in between that is put out. So do yourself a favor and stop dwelling in fear. Have courage and confidence to act in spite of fear and eventually live fearlessly. A fearless person is not a person who doesn't have any fearful thoughts. A fearless person is one whose desires are so strong that all their fearful thoughts are insignificant, and they choose faithful thoughts.

Is there something that you always wanted to do or be, but talked yourself out of doing because of fear?

If there was a guarantee that you will not fail, what will you do, be, and have? (List all things)

What is the worst that can happen if you tried it now? Don't just write "I will fail."

Meditation: Fearless

I breathe in confidence and breathe out all fear.

I am strong enough to overcome any fear in my life.

I am never alone. God is always with me.

God's power operates through me and makes me feel free and fearless.

I am not afraid, I know my inner-being guides me.

I face my fears and rise above them.

Fear is nothing but an emotion that I choose to dismiss.

I am in control of my life.

The courage in my heart dissolves any fears I may feel.

I act in spite of the fear and the fear fades away.

I am stronger than any fear.

I am finally free from all disempowering fears and doubts

Section 2: Money

"One step toward financial literacy takes you two steps toward personal empowerment."

– Russell Simmons

Money Is Evil
Fuck Believing

Money is not evil. I repeat: MONEY IS NOT EVIL. Good and evil are in the thoughts, motivation, and actions of men. A dollar is a piece of paper. If a dollar is evil, the clothes on your back are evil too because the dollar is made from the same material: cotton. Let's not forget those evil little coins: copper, uranium, silver, lead, and nickel. Oooh, those evil, little materials! Doesn't that sound absurd! Before the almighty, green dollar came to pass, people paid for services with food, tea, weapons, and even human skulls. Truth be told, if the means of currency were cockroaches, then people will kill over cockroaches.

All that being said, don't mix the energy of money with the energy of the humans handling it wrongfully. If you do hold the belief that money is evil, you hold a condemning thought of money and that thought alone will keep it away from you. It's up to you and your beliefs about money to determine how easily it flows to you. If you have a positive relationship with money, it will flow easily to you. If you have a negative relationship with money, you are blocking the frequency of money easily flowing to you.

There is not a God in the sky that looks down on people and says, you can have more abundance and points to another and says you can have more abundance. You, naw, no more abundance for you. You, right there, here goes more for you. You, over there, hell no, you can't get any of this. You, right there, you, cool, here you go. You, nope, no more abundance for you. If you believe there is a God that wants you to live this life miserably, unhappily, or just getting by until you die and finally be happy when you get to heaven, then that's exactly what you'll do. God wants you to be happy. But God wants you to choose what you will get out of life. Our choices are made out of our beliefs. So look at your life, and ask yourself is this the life I want. If it's not, it's time to find out what beliefs you possess that's keeping you away from your desires. You can have it all: a great relationship, good health, and you can have an abundance of money!

Can you think of any limiting beliefs you heard as a kid about money that you may be holding on to?

Write down the blessings associated with money?

1.	**2.**
3.	**4.**
5.	**6.**
7.	**8.**
9.	**10.**
11.	**12.**
13.	**14.**
15.	**16.**
17.	**18.**
19.	**20.**

Meditation: Abundance

God is the source of everything.

God's wealth flows to me joyously and freely.

God is my instant supply.

I am advancing and growing mentally, spiritually and financially.

My faith in God means I have faith in all things good.

Every day I am becoming more and more open to receiving the great abundance of the universe.

I allow great abundance to flow in all areas of my life.

Today I reclaim the abundance that is my universal right.

It is perfectly alright for me to expect an abundant life.

I deserve to receive great abundance in my life.

I move forward with an expectancy of great abundance in my life.

Lack of Money

Fuck Lacking Money

Do you want more money? Do you believe you can have more money? Is your subconscious mind in agreement with your conscious desire of wanting money? Are there programs in your subconscious mind that are not in alignment with having more money? There are a lot of people who are not aware that they are holding themselves back from having more money because they accepted the beliefs that money is evil, money comes hard, money doesn't grow on trees, money comes few and far between, only dishonest people make money, money corrupts everyone, you can't make money doing what you love, money isn't important to me, I don't do this for the money, I am happy with what I have I don't need a lot. Any negative view of money can keep money from coming to you.

Everyone says they want money and based on the premise that words have power, a lot of people ask, "Why don't I have more money because I say I want more money?" If you agreed with the proposed question, then that is one reason why you don't have more money. You are focused on NOT HAVING more. You get whatever you focus on. If you are focused on the fact that you DON'T have more, you WON'T have more. Now I can't say specifically what you are doing to hold more money away from you because I don't know you personally, but I'm going to start with the fact that many people ask the previous question. But the true question is, do you believe that you can have more money?

You can think about wanting more all you want.

But, unless your subconscious mind holds the BELIEF that you can have an abundance of money, you won't have an abundance. How can you know the belief that your subconscious mind holds? You can tell by your feelings when the topic of money is brought up. Do you get sad most times when you think about it? Do you get angry when thinking about spending? Do you beat yourself up for not having enough? Do you feel hopeless when you think about having more or do you feel inspired and faithful?

If you continue to give your energy to your current situation, you're going to get more of your current situation. With that being said, if you look at your life and think, *my poor life,* you will get more poorness in your life. If you look at your life and think, *my blessed life*, you will get more blessings in life. It is that simple. Even when you judge another person's life, you are impacting your very own life based on your perception. If you see a homeless person and can fix your lips to say "poor guy," you have the capacity of being poor.

If you look at someone on TV and shake your head and say, "It's ridiculous that he has all that money," then you are limiting the amount of money that you can have. Again, you go where your energy goes.

You have to release old beliefs about money and start believing in plenty. You have to believe that you are just as worthy of having it like the people that do have it. You are just as special as they are. A lot of people want to dumb it down and say, "I don't need all that money, I just want to live comfortably." That's another way of saying, "I don't think I can have a lot of money, so I'll take a little bit."

If someone came to you with 500 million dollars and says, "You can have it all or give me a specific amount," you are not going to say, "Let me just get five million because I just want to be comfortable." You're going to take all of it. The only reason people claim they don't need a lot and they just want to be comfortable is because that's the limit of their belief on what they can have or should have. You are holding yourself back from the abundance that God promises you can have.

I don't want to get too hung up on money, but money is the primary thing that people relate to their happiness. Money should make you happy. Money should make you have a feeling of happiness just like a kiss from a significant other, or the smell of a rose, or a day out on the beach, or playing with a pet, or a good long relieving bowel movement. So, yes, it's okay to believe that money can make you happy. Should it determine the value of your life? NO, but there is value in money! If you think it's something wrong with saying money makes you happy, maybe we found the belief that's holding you away from it. Your belief about anything reflects the capacity to whether you can attain it or not. Your health should make you happy, your relationships should make you happy, your career should make you happy, and so why can't you say money makes you happy.

Let me note that having an abundance of money does not mean you will feel complete. Just because money can bring some happy experiences doesn't mean it will bring a sound mind, a peaceful state of being, and a feeling of fulfillment. Again, money is just like any other thing that can bring happiness. A walk in the park can bring happiness, but a person can still feel depressed when they walk out of the park. A piece of pizza can bring happiness, but that piece of pizza will not make one feel fulfilled if one is battling with self-love. So if you are looking to have more money to feel fulfilled, you will feel emptier than ever, because money is not the solution to that problem. Money is just another experience that comes and goes.

Release money freely. Accept money freely. It is not the end all be all in life. The best thing in life is free: Love. Focus on the things money can't buy to get your energy flowing towards feeling good, so good things can flow to you. If you are not in a positive place with money, focus on something else. I know it may be a challenging task because the bills won't stop, the food has to be bought, and the roof has to remain over your head. But guess what... Those things will be there regardless of your stress or peace. So what is the point of stressing? One thing's for sure, your stressing won't change your situation. Do you know what will? Peace.

On this earth, money is a way to demonstrate the power that God gave us. You don't have to wait until you die and get to heaven in order to live happily and abundantly. Don't get it twisted, I'm not saying that you need money to be happy. What I'm saying is, God wants us to live like royalty because that's who he is and we are a reflection of him. He wants us to have abundance because that's who he is and we are a reflection of him. He just gives us the choice to live in abundance and that choice starts in your mind.

How much money do you want to have? Why did you choose that number?

Do you believe you can have the amount of money you desire? Why or why not?

What do you have to do to start getting more money than you have?

Meditation: Money

I love and appreciate money and what it can do.

All the money I desire is flowing into my life.

I am in charge of my financial situation.

I believe that money makes wonderful things happen.

I improve my life and the life of others by having lots of money to spend.

Money is a positive resource.

I deserve to have a debt-free life.

I am grateful for all the money I have in my life now.

I have the power to transform my money-thoughts into income.

My appreciation for money is multiplying the money.
I have in my life.
I have a loving relationship with money.
I know there is enough money in the world for everyone including myself.

Section 3: Letting Go

"We must develop and maintain the capacity to forgive. He who is devoid of the power to forgive is devoid of the power to love. There is some good in the worst of us and some evil in the best of us. When we discover this, we are less prone to hate our enemies."

– Martin Luther King Jr.

Past Mistakes

Fuck Letting Your Past Mistakes Beat You Up

Oh, this one right here! Listen it's a process to forgive yourself and let go of the past. When I say the past, I mean literally from ONE second ago – on back. Once you truly forgive yourself from your past fuck ups, that's when you make a big stride in the process of self-love. Self-love is an ongoing practice. The first step is getting over your guilt, shame, and embarrassment if you are harboring any of those feelings. You know that no one is perfect, so don't expect yourself to be perfect. You may have fucked up in the past, but you don't have to keep fucking up. You may have done some fucked up shit to someone, but that doesn't mean you have to keep doing fucked up shit. You may have fucked someone who didn't deserve your love, but that doesn't mean you have to continue to keep fucking people that don't deserve it…

Forgive yourself and grow. If someone can't move on from you fucking them over in the past and they don't forgive you, that's their burden, don't continue to make it yours. When you ask for forgiveness and you truly changed your ways, you are forgiven by God and ultimately that's all that matters. While you're here on earth, you may feel like you need others to forgive you to make you feel whole again, but I'm telling you God's forgiveness is the only forgiveness needed. So forgive yourself and ask others for forgiveness if you feel compelled. I ask for forgiveness from those who fell victim to pain caused by me during my days of self-hate. I used to be in a place where I didn't give a fuck about myself so I was in no shape to give a fuck about anybody else for that matter. I have said some bogus things to people, put my hands on a few, and done some things that I wouldn't do again. I don't have to dive into specifics because it was so long ago, high school and college, I'm not the same person I was yesterday, so I for damn sure have grown since being a teen and young adult. Hopefully, if anyone feels some ill-will toward me, you find it in your heart to forgive, if not I can truly say I don't give a fuck, I forgave myself and love myself and I wish the same for all.

I have to note that depending on what you did, you cannot expect everyone to move on from the pain you caused. You have to find a way to push through your past though. You have to find a way to understand that most of your programming came from sources outside of yourself. Violence, abuse, and all other negativities are passed down generationally and socially. Make no excuses though. Own up, grow up, and move on. It is time to become your own you and release things that you were taught that are not you anymore. If you truly are a better person, find a way to let go of your past and forgive yourself. Then if it is in your reach, teach others that you see are like the old you, so they won't fall victim to your same mistakes.

What past mistake(s) haunts you? If you don't have any, take the time to praise yourself for that!

Write down something that makes you happy, smile, or laugh.

Let this be the last time you mention that mistake you wrote to anyone or yourself. As soon as you think about that mistake, think about the thing you wrote that makes you happy, smile, or laugh.

Meditation: Releasing the Past

I forgive myself for every unkind thing I have done in the past.

I forgive myself totally and unconditionally.

I empower my life by forgiving and releasing.

I choose to let go of the past, and embrace the present moment.

I am willing to let go of my past and take the next step towards a better future.

I apologize to myself for living in the past.

I am now living my life without regret because I cherish the present.

I am now beyond my past.

Every day I am letting go of everything that has been holding me back.

By forgiving myself and others I set myself free.

Forgiving but Not Forgetting

Fuck Forgiving Without Forgetting

Since we talked about forgiving the self, it's only right that we dive into forgiving others. We know you won't forget when you've been wronged. It's pretty much mentally impossible to forget because our subconscious mind remembers everything, especially events deemed as important or traumatic, but you don't have to choose to think about the events. So yes, you won't forget after forgiving, I get that. BUT you don't have to walk around reminding yourself about a negative situation. Now I'm not saying go and be friends with someone you don't want to be friends with, but let go of the past. Forgive and move on whether it's with or without the person. If you do decide to keep a relationship with a person who fucked you over, that person doesn't want to keep hearing you say, "I forgive you, but remember when you did this."

"I forgive you but I'll never forget when you did that."

That person gone eventually feel like "fuck your forgiveness if I have to keep going through this!" Not only are you making that person feel bad for past mistakes, you are also making yourself feel bad when you constantly think about the thing that hurt you. Constantly side-eyeing, talking shit, or looking for the next fuck up won't help you get over it. Furthermore, if you feel that person hasn't changed, then you don't need to be holding on anyway.

To get away from the topic of relationships, it is important to forgive anyone who has hurt you. I was asked by my significant other, "What about child molesters? What about a murderer? Should they be forgiven?" Man, as much as I would like to say no fuck them! That's not my place. Only the creator can judge, not me or you. If you have experienced anyone like that personally, I pray for your heart's freedom. I pray that you let go of hate because hate taints the person carrying it, not the person that is being hated. When you condemn you are being condemned, so you have to forgive and move on. It doesn't mean you have to like the person. It doesn't mean you condoning what the person did. It means you are letting go of resentment and judgment.

If you were subjected to any form of abuse, I pray you are not defining your life based on your pain, hurt, confusion, and wounds. You cannot allow yourself to be controlled by your abuser's failures. From my personal knowledge, many (not all) people that commit abuse have been abused. Those people needed help. Those people never dealt with pain. Those people never forgave people that hurt them. If you have not recovered and you hold feelings of victimization, please reach out to a professional and talk with them about how you are feeling. Forgiveness is not about the abuser. It's not your job to make his life better by knowing you forgave. Hell, he/she doesn't even have to know you are forgiving and letting go. When forgiveness occurs, a person is set free and that person is you, the victim.

No one can tell you when to forgive. If you are a victim you have been through a lot, so it's understandable why you feel the way you do. But you owe it to yourself to be free! (For those who haven't been a victim of abuse, excuse me going off on a tangent. Someone reading this may have needed to read it).

If you are not in a place of forgiveness, fuck forgiving. The most important thing to do is heal. If you have been hurt mentally, physically, or sexually, please seek help. If you don't, you can end up like the person who has hurt you-sick. I'm not saying you will do the things your abuser has done to you. Although there are many who do turn out to be just like their abuser, especially children. What I am referring to is the fact that you can become physically and mentally sick. Traumatic experiences affect your neurobiological system. There is a study called the ACE study that investigated childhood abuse, neglect, and household challenges effects on later-life health. The results are astonishing. In short, there is a direct correlation between adverse childhood experiences and negative health outcomes that include depression, anxiety, alcohol and drug abuse, suicide, cancer and diabetes. This is not only true for children, if you experience a traumatic even as an adult that stress can affect you in a negative way. You can develop either a mental or physical illness as a direct result of adversity. You didn't get yourself in your situation, so you don't have to try to get yourself out of it. It is okay to need help. Many people don't want to admit it, but we can all use someone to lean on. Please lean on someone you can trust, that will bring you safety, and that can help you get through whatever it is that you are going through.

Is there anyone you need to forgive?

Do you need to forgive yourself for shame or negative self-perception caused by someone else? If yes, for what?

The FBI has a number of resources for victims of crime if you need support. Here are a few:
National Center for Victims of Crime: (800) 394-2255
www.ncvc.org

National Organization for Victim Assistance :(800) 879-6682 www.trynova.org

National Organization of Parents of Murdered Children: (888) 818-7662 www.pomc.com

Rape, Abuse and Incest National Network: (800) 656-4673 www.rainn.org

Meditation: Forgiveness

I forgive and forget easily because I know that nobody is perfect.
I relinquish all attachment to past pain.
I forgive myself for all ill feelings I have harbored in the past.
I release all past pain, and welcome new space and freedom in my life.

I forgive all people in my life, including myself.

I release all resentment and now see things from an enlightened perspective.

I know that releasing the past, I heal.

I forgive and forget the past and welcome the present.

I freely release the need to hold anything over anyone's head.

I release every negative experience from my past.

I let go and move on.

Section 4: Believing

"Yes, We Can!"

– Barack Obama

Doubt

Fuck Doubt

The answer to a prayer is already in the prayer when it is prayed. If when you pray, you are praying doubtfully thinking it won't happen, then that is the answer to your prayer: it won't happen. If you are guessing if your prayer will be answered, the answer to that prayer will be up in the air and continuously having you guessing. See your word as truth and get rid of doubt. Be peaceful and confident. Don't look for results because that's doubting. Don't be anxious and start wondering when it will happen for you because that's doubting.

Here is how you pray:

Say your prayer. Know that your word was heard. Know that your word is truth. And know what you want is accomplished. Then go about your day.

Out of all the questions in the world. What? Why? How? When? Where? Who? Will? You can confidently answer two of them when it is dealing with something that you want to manifest. You can answer WHAT you want and you can answer WHY you want it. That's it. You may think you know when it will happen. You may think you know where it will happen. You may think you know who it will happen with. You may think you know how it will happen. But the only thing you know for sure is what you want and why you want it. Most times when people try to answer the other questions and don't know the answers, doubt starts to creep in.

Those answers are for God to answer. You focus on what you can, and let God do the rest, and don't keep asking God when is it going to happen for me? When is it my turn?

Imagine if you had a child that comes up to you on Monday and says, "Can you take me to the amusement park?"

You say, "Yes, I will take you on Saturday."

On Tuesday the child comes back and asks, "Can you take me to the amusement park?"

You say, "Yes, on Saturday."

The child comes again on Wednesday and says, "Will you take me to the amusement park?"

You say, "I already told you yes, on Saturday I'll take you."

On Thursday the child comes back and says, "Are we going to the amusement park?"

You say, "Oh, my God, if you come and ask me again, I'm not taking you. Leave me alone."

On Friday the child comes back. You see where this is going. It's leading to irritation. It's leading to you not even wanting to take the kid to the amusement park. Not saying that God is getting irritated or will stop you from getting what you want just to prove a point. But every time you ask for something in a prayer, then ask again. Then ask again and again. You are displaying doubt. Not faith. Stop asking for the same thing. Let it come to you.

Is there something or someone in your life you have prayed about more than one time? If yes, write it down.

What do you want? Why do you want it?

Now let go and let God. Stop doubting. Stop asking. Have faith and let it come.

Meditation: Releasing Doubt

I choose to believe only those thoughts which empower my life.

I quickly release all emotions that impede my progress.

I release beliefs that are in conflict with my desires.

I release all old beliefs and create new supportive ones.

I release the need to second guess my abilities.

I am confident in myself and my abilities.

I believe in myself.

I choose to fill my mind with empowering, positive thoughts.

I easily get rid of all beliefs that no longer serve me.

I accept only positive thoughts, feelings, and actions.

I choose to focus my mind on uplifting thoughts.

This Is Too Good to Be True

Fuck "This Is Too Good to Be True"

It's like we are so used to not having good things, we can't believe it when we do have them. A "it's too good to be true" mentality shouldn't be anyone's way of thinking, but the reality is it is the normal mentality for many. Start disbelieving in the bad instead of disbelieving in the good. We need to make it the norm to have good, be good, smell good, do good, live good, everything good that we don't have to have a shock factor when something good does come along. Let's tilt the scale to make the good side heavier.

A "this is too good to be true" mentality brings you things that are too good to be true. Which in turn makes you believe that things are too good to be true.

You say, "I knew it was too good to be true." However, your belief in that statement is the reason you got that thing in the very first place. The cause is your belief that you can't have good. The effect is you receiving the bad: too good to be true. People who walk around thinking that things are too good to be true for them is another way of saying, you don't think you deserve good. Or you simply don't know that you can attract good into your life.

Once you drop that mentality, you will receive all the things that you believe are too good to be true. You have every right to receive the "too good to be true" lover. You have every right to receive the "too good to be true" job. You have every right to receive the "too good to be true" friendship. You have every right to receive an abundance of goodness because it is your birthright. Stop stripping the goodness away from yourself with your limited beliefs. Own all the goodness that comes into your life. It is yours! You deserve it, it's not too good to be true!

What is an ideal relationship?

What is an ideal financial status?

What is an ideal life?

Do you think you can have everything that is ideal? Why or why not?

Meditation: Feeling Good Enough to Have Good

I am as capable of success as anyone else.
I deserve to have the life I want.

I have what it takes.

I was born in the image of God: successful, confident, and worthy.

Success is my birthright and I accept this birthright now.

I am a wonderful person so I attract wonderful things.

I am as valid and important as anyone else.

I am learning to love myself more and more each and every day.

Every day I am growing and appreciate who I am becoming.

I deserve the best of everything.

Section 5: Negative People

Never be limited by other people's limited imaginations. If you adopt their attitudes, then the possibility won't exist because you'll have already shut it out... You can hear other people's wisdom, but you've got to re-evaluate the world for yourself.

– Mae Jemison

The Disbelievers
Fuck the Disbelievers

People will try to talk you out of doing something because they talked themselves out of doing something. I asked 50 people if they wish they would have done something that they have never done. Can you guess the number of people that said yes? All 50! Those desires, or regrets as some worded it, were writing a book, visiting different countries, being a singer, going to college, having more than one kid, opening a restaurant, investing, and the list goes on.

Why, oh, why would you listen to someone else telling you not to do something, when most people you encounter don't commit to their own desires? You have to listen to yourself. You and only you can tell you what is best for you. But let me make this clear, you have to be clear about the root of your inner messages. Sometimes you can't even listen to yourself because it depends on the source of where your message comes from even within yourself. You have to remember that our brain holds beliefs that are from other people, so you may be getting other people's negative messages that were downloaded into you.

Listen to your soul. Your inner being will guide you and you won't go wrong. Fuck other people's beliefs, most people don't even believe in themselves. Successful people will tell you that you can succeed and give you logical reasons why they think you wouldn't. Unsuccessful, fearful people will just convince you, you will fail just because they are fearful, they feel like your goal is unattainable to them, or because they have once failed at it. Your job is to commit to your desire then focus on what feels good from there.

If you don't have clarity, be still. Don't make moves in a confused state. Be still by meditating and opening yourself up to the guidance from the Most High. Pray and ask for clarity, the answer will come to you if you open yourself to receiving it. The best way to be open to an answer coming to you is by being in a peaceful state. It is hard to hear anything if you feel bothered, distressed, and down. Think about those times in your life when you have felt negative, you don't' even want to be bothered with anyone else. So, lean in to good feeling things and allow what you are looking for to enter into your life.

Honestly, it's really best to keep your idea to yourself until you wholeheartedly believe in it so much that no one else can come in and change your mind about it. Don't give people an opportunity to pour doubt into your desires. Once you have reached that point, it won't matter what anyone else's opinion is about what was placed in your heart. The most important thing to remember is that your vision is not going to be seen by everyone. Learn to be okay with that. The people who see your vision are the ones that will motivate you, support you, or be a part of it.

Has anyone ever told you that something was hard to do?

Do you know anyone (personally or not personally) that has succeeded at what you want to do?

What is the difference between you and the person who has succeeded at what you want?

Meditation: Courage to Do What Others Can't Do

I am confident that I have what it takes to reach my goals.

Many people have accomplished that I want to accomplish.

I am worthy of receiving my desires.

The opinions of others have no bearing on how I feel about myself.

Every day I am becoming more and more courageous.

I am strong, bold, and courageous.

I boldly go in the direction of my dreams.

Within me is all the courage I need to reach my potential.

I have the courage to overcome all difficulties in my life.

I have what it takes to accomplish my goals.

I trust my ability to face all of life's challenges.

They Sayers

Fuck the "They Sayers"

Earlier in the book, I said I would get to the "They Sayers." They say is used to state what people in general say or think. They say it's bad luck to spill salt. They say you shouldn't put your purse on the floor because you'll be broke. They say fatherless children are more prone to commit crime. They say it's better to be poor and happy than rich and miserable. Listen, stop listening to what they say, and listen to what I say. LOL. For real though, if you listen to everything people say without testing it, questioning it, thinking about it, you are open to just believing other people's false beliefs. It's limiting to take one person's truth and make it yours just because it existed for them. You need to make yourself knowledgeable so you can handle your own situation according to you, not according to anyone else.

Knowledge is power and is key to discerning if what they say holds any power. Get your own understanding of certain situations. What they say may be beneficial but then again what they say may not be beneficial. A creative person is driven by curiosity and wonderment. If you want to create your own life and reality you have to gain your own understanding. You learn more by looking for answers instead of allowing people to answer things for you. You have to have confidence in your own intelligence. I'm not saying you have to walk around disbelieving everything you hear nor am I saying everything you hear is false. I am saying there are some falsities that are spread and people readily accept them. If people didn't venture away from what they say, discoveries wouldn't be made and new changes would never occur.

The first change can be within you. You are who you are based on what "they said" to you as you were learning who you were in this world. Your parents, teachers, friends (your environment) molding you to think, be, and act out who you are. If you question why you do everything you do, you will gain insight into the source of your habits. If you question why you think everything you think, you will gain insight into the source of your thoughts. People are comfortable just being who they were molded to be, trusting that everything they were told from parents, news, and friends is factual. People really believe that every habit they have is "just them."

Start questioning the opinions of those that influenced your opinions and you will gain knowledge of who you truly are. Don't be afraid to change something you so easily accepted. You have the right to question. That's how kids gain knowledge and that is how you can continue to gain knowledge. That's how you will truly know if what they say is valid.

From whom did you learn the concept of success?

What is the belief that you hold about relationships that may be based on one perception or experience?

Meditation: Knowledge

As I relax into each situation in my life, I receive divine wisdom.

I am always open to wisdom and learning.

I am constantly improving my understanding of things.

I have free access to the infinite powers of my mind.

The wisdom I seek is forever within me.

I feed my mind with new ideas and understanding daily.

I have the necessary intelligence to do all that I desire.

My inner being is connected to the limitless wisdom of the universe.

I am always open to improvement.

I am gaining knowledge and wisdom at all times.

Section 6
You Are a Co-Creator

"The most common way people give up their power is by thinking they don't have any."

– Alice Walker

Powers Outside of God and Yourself

Fuck Believing in Powers Outside of God and Yourself

Alright, now listen. Nobody or nothing. Let me say that again, NOBODY or NOTHING has the power to make you do anything unless you give the power to them. Even if you give someone the ability to have power over your life, that is still you using your POWER of choice. There is no evil spirit going around on this earth making people snort drugs, steal, kill, or whatever else you may consider evil. There isn't such thing as a curse, a jinx, voodoo, or whatever other thing people account for their wrongdoings or failures. But there are such things if you BELIEVE there are because whatever you believe you receive. Say, for instance, a grandmother tells her grandchild that the family is cursed. If the child believes it, the child will grow up disbelieving in herself, thinking something has control over her destiny, so she most likely won't put her best foot forward and conquer her fears. Which will, in turn, cause her to continue "failing" and not achieving what she wishes which will, in turn, make her believe that the curse was real. When it really was only her belief in the curse that was real.

Evil will disappear if everyone chooses to do good. Yes, we do have a choice to act righteously or to act wrongly. When the entire world CHOOSES right, then we won't see any evil period. Wrongdoings, crimes, wickedness, corruption, and lawbreaking are all choices, not some evil force, boogie man, hidden entity floating through people. If you believe it is, then so be it, you are right and you are powerless as well.

God gave us the power of creation and choices. You can create the life you want to have through the choices that you make. Some people will argue that we don't truly have choices because we only get to choose from the opportunities that exist. Let me remind you that you can create more opportunities to choose from. If Martin Luther King Junior chose to accept the choices that was given to him, African Americans wouldn't have had an advancement in civil rights. If Elizabeth Stanton and Susan Anthony only made choices from the options they had, women wouldn't have the right to vote. If something you want doesn't exist, create it. Do not sit back a think you are powerless. Do not sit back and think that someone else or something else has power over you. You can create the change that you want to see by using the power invested you by God. You can be the person you want to be by the power invested in you by God.

What or who drains your energy? Why do you ALLOW it to happen?

What or who can make you "act out of character?" Why do you allow it to happen?

You were not born with a remote. Stop letting people control you!

Meditation: Self-Empowerment

Connections with my inner spirit bring me peace.

Every moment I am becoming more and more empowered.

I am always connected to my creator.

I am connected to my higher being at all times.

I have the ability to change anything in my life.

I am one with the universal mind.

I am power.

I embrace the feeling of being an infinite spirit.

Divine power is within me and it creates miracles in my life.

The Force is within me, and this force is unlimited.

Every day in every way I am getting better and better.

I am constantly evolving into the best person I can be.

I am ready and able to improve my life.

Creating Your Own Reality
Fuck Making Other's Reality Your Reality

The reality is there are some people who are poor. The reality is there are some people who are rich. The reality is there are some people who are safe and sound. The reality is there are some people who are harmed. The reality is there are some people who die young. The reality is there are some people who die old. The reality is there are some people that die old suffering. The reality is there are some people who die old peacefully. The reality is there are some people that failed. The reality is there are some people that succeeded. The reality is there are some people who are healthy. The reality is there are some people who are not sickly. The reality is there are some people who fall but get up. The reality is there are some people who fall and stay down. The reality is there are some positives. The reality is there are some negatives.

The reality is whatever, and I mean WHATEVER, you focus on and give your ENERGY to (talking about, thinking about, reading about) you will attract into your life. Choose your reality by choosing which reality you give your energy to because the reality is; you choose your reality!

Unless you are taking the positives from others in life and making it yours, stop making other people's reality your reality. The world is full of good, take the good and let go of everything else. Yes, bad exist, but you have a choice of what you focus on. You have a choice of what you think about. You have a choice of what you talk about. You have a choice of what you be about. Choose to focus on the good because it will attract more good into your life.

As I stated earlier, I know that we are all born into different circumstances. The reality is your reality doesn't have to remain the same. I understand that it is an anomaly for a person to go from rags to riches. More people stay in rags when they come from rags. The common denominator for those people who made something out of nothing was their strong desire to have more and something different, along with dedication and determination. They kept on choosing to do things that would create a difference. They kept on going when things looked rough. They did not give up. They may have stopped and felt like it was too hard to keep going, but they got going again. They kept their heart and energy focused on their desire. I know this is going to sound cliché, but I am going to say it anyway. If one person can do it, so can you. They are special, but they are not any more special than you are. Create your new reality if you are not pleased with the one you have. In order to do that, you have to focus on what you want your new reality to be, not focus on what your reality is.

What do you believe about money, relationships, growing older, other races?

Why do you believe in your beliefs?

Meditation: Choosing Your Own Reality

I am in control of my life.

I am creating my perfect life one thought at a time.

I choose to welcome all the good things life has to offer.

I look for and welcome all the pleasure of life.

I only acknowledge the best in life.

I treasure my life as it is now and this will bring me more treasure in my life.

My heart is open to receive all the joy that life has to offer.

My life is improving in countless ways.

My life just keeps getting better and better.

Today I choose to be aware of the beauty of life.

Today I will look for a reason to smile.

Section 7: Self-Confidence

"Nobody is going to love you like you. You're going to be your best salesman."

– T.I.

Be You

Fuck Trying to Be Like
Someone Else: Be You

The way one person accomplished something is not the only way. Your journey is specifically made for you. When you try to do it like someone else, to be like someone else, you will most likely fail. Don't get me wrong. You can be motivated and inspired by others, but you can never be them. Don't try the be the next Beyonce, Michael Phelps, or LeBron James. There is no such thing as the next of any of them. They are who they are and you can only be who you are. You can be great at what you do and set your own records and put your own imprints in this world.

Work to be the best you. You can only be great at being you, not at being someone else. You can read a million books and still not write a great book if it's not for you. You can imitate a great singer and still not sing good if it is not for you. Trying to live up to other people's standards will not feel fulfilling because once you think you conquered someone else's accomplishments, you will look for something/someone else to be better than just to make you feel accomplished. Go hard because you want to be better, not because you want to be better than someone else. People always want to compare and contrast. It's okay for more than one person to be great, even if it is at the same time. Focus on you. You can be the shit without shitting on others. Stay humble. Stay grounded.

Create yourself. Use your gifts and you will inevitably succeed. Discover your life's purpose if you have not already figured it out. Your life's purpose is something that makes you happy. When you are living out your life's purpose, you do it effortlessly because it draws from your strengths and talents. It gives you a feeling of fulfillment. Listening to your feelings and emotions will keep you on track as you live out your life's purpose. If you are experiencing positive feelings, then you are tuned in. If you are experiencing negativity, you are not lined up with your life's purpose. Allow your feelings to guide and keep you on the right path.

It may not be a smooth path, but those rough patches will help you know for sure if you are walking in your purpose. You will be driven to get past hurdles because you know the outcome is going to be worth every step you have to take to get there. Challenges will come in all shapes and forms on any day of the week. The day you realize life comes with things that will feel uneasy to you, will be the day you can overcome them a little easier. Think about the fact that in order to bring life into this world, women go through the challenge of giving birth. Think about babies going through sleepless nights teething and then those two beautiful teeth finally appear. Just because something is not easy doesn't mean it has to be a negative experience. You can get through challenges and "pain" for the gain of accomplishing your goals.

Is there something that you are always complimented on?

What talents do you have? How can you enhance your talents?

What is your life's purpose? (Write ANYTHING that comes to you. If you can't come up with something, keep asking yourself the question.

Meditation: Purpose

I follow my own true path and let others follow theirs.

As I grow more connected to my soul, my life's purpose becomes clearer.

Every day I strive to embrace my life's true purpose.

I choose to direct my thoughts and actions towards my purpose.

I am creating a life of passion and purpose.

I know that I was born into this world to fulfill an important and unique purpose.

I trust my purpose to lead me towards happiness and well-being.

I welcome inspiration and clarity into my life.

My life purpose guides and directs me in all that I do.

My life purpose is extremely important to me and deserves my full effort and attention.

Trying to Look Like Others

Fuck Trying to Look Like Someone Else

Defining your beauty based on the way someone else looks is self-destruction. When you compare yourself to another and start doubting yourself, you FEAR you are not beautiful. Yet, you are beautifully made. God made EVERYONE in his image. Every North American, South American, African, Asian, European, and Australian, and so on were made in God's image. So love who you are and stop allowing others to define your beauty. More importantly, stop hating the way God made you because you are one of his prized creations. For those that hate others that that don't look like you, you are basically telling God he made a mistake for not making everyone the same as you.

In my admission letter to grad school, they wanted me to talk about diversity. In that letter, I discussed how for some odd reason, diversity creates a need for people to compare and contrast themselves to others. When we compare ourselves to one another it can cause self-hate or hatred toward another. Keeping that in mind, it is important to teach people not to hate others because of differences. Needless to say, the root of hate comes from the inability to accept people for who they are. A blonde may think she is better than a brunette, a skinny person may think he looks better than a fat person, a Catholic may feel better than a Christian, and so on. When someone hates someone else's hair, that means the hateful person feels the other person's hair should meet a certain standard. The same goes for someone who hates someone else's choice of attire, career, spouse, and so forth. When it's all said and done, the moment people learn how to allow diversity, hate will diminish. We are born without hate in our hearts. People are taught to hate diversity. Therefore, acceptance of diversity needs to be taught.

At the same time, it is important to teach self-love because one can view his own differences in a negative way. Once the masses' perception of diversity is turned from negative to positive, more people fall in love with life and the uniqueness it brings. Moreover, more people will fall in love with themselves because people won't hate themselves for not being like other people they were taught they should be like. Self-hate is the worst hate of them all in my opinion. Self-hate can lead to hate towards others because it can be hard to be loving and kind to others if one is not loving and kind to self. Once a person is able to love themselves unconditionally, he or she most likely will not jeopardize his own happiness, freedom, and life by doing hateful things toward themselves or others. Be proud of who you are and allow others to be who they are without making comparisons.

By what standards do you judge yourself?

Do you love yourself?
If you love yourself, good! But, ask someone else that question because he/she may be struggling with self-love. I asked one of my loved ones this question after I typed this question, "Do you love what you see when you look in the mirror?" and she broke down crying. You never know what people are going through on the inside.

If you don't love yourself, you are not alone. Call someone and talk about it. Don't listen to the voice in your head telling you not to. Call someone. It can be a hotline if you don't want to talk to someone you know.

Meditation: Self-Acceptance

I love the person I am becoming.
I love myself.
I see myself as a beautiful expression of life.
I treat myself like the divine being I am.
I love the new, abundant me.
I love being me.
I love myself more each day.
I know that my true nature is perfect in every way.
I know my true self and love it unconditionally.
I give myself all the compassion I deserve and need.
I feel very special because I love and respect myself.
I embrace myself.

Section 8
Healthy Relationships

"Do not bring people in your life who weigh you down. And trust your instincts...good relationships feel good. They feel right. They don't hurt. They're not painful. That's not just with somebody you want to marry, but it's with the friends that you choose. It's with the people you surround yourselves with."

– Michelle Obama

Ex-Boos

Fuck Your Ex-Boo

Not literally, your ex is an ex for a reason. If it didn't work out, you need to move ahead and move along and don't dip back. Unless your ex has evolved like you have. Don't take the same person back. You broke up for a reason. Most times, we stay in unhealthy relationships because we don't know our worth, so we get someone that doesn't treat us worthy. We stay in unhealthy relationships because we FEAR we will never get anyone else. We fear no one else will want us the way the ex did. We fear we are running out of time. All of those things are untrue.

What's more untrue is the statement: love hurts! I'm not sure who started that bullshit but release that belief immediately. Hate hurts. Love feels good. Beatings hurt. Love is kind. Lies hurt. Love is comforting. Abandonment hurts. Love is embracing. Love is forgiving. Love is selfless. Selfishness hurts. Love is unconditional and protects. If you're not experiencing feelings of greatness, you are not experiencing love at that moment.

Relationships will have its ups and downs, but you should have far more ups. I'm not talking a 50/50 split either. You need to have far more positive feelings and

91

experiences than negative feelings and experiences in your relationship. If it is the opposite, you are far from what you deserve. You need to be with someone that is going to bring out your greatness. Matter of fact, you don't need anyone to bring out anything. You need someone that knows their own greatness, so they won't stop you from being great. You need to be with someone that is not looking for a "better half." They should be a complete whole looking for another complete whole so that when you all come together you all are completely secure, content, and happy in yourselves and can help keep each other in that vibration.

So if your ex is the same draining, bitter, broke without a drive, negative, insecure person, leave them where they belong. In your past. Moving forward, make sure you are in a new place because you will get another one of your ex's in a different body if you are not. It's a reason why you attracted your ex at the time you attracted your ex. Let your next boo be a reflection of your growth. Let your next love be a reflection of your happiness. You deserve to have a great, happy, positive relationship if you are being a great, happy, positive person.

Why is your last ex your ex?

What did you learn about yourself from a previous relationship?

What are 20 qualities that are important to you in a mate? (Why settle for anything less?)

1.	2.
3.	4.
5.	6.
7.	8.
9.	10.
11.	12.
13.	14.
15.	16.
17.	18.
19.	20.

Meditation: Healthy Love Life

I am a love magnet.

I expect my ideal mate to appear in my life anytime.

I am now ready to accept a happy, fulfilling relationship.

Men/women find me attractive and sexy.

I deserve to find my perfect soul mate.

I accept a perfect loving relationship with open arms.

I allow love to find me easily and effortlessly.

I am making room in my life for my perfect other half.

I am ready to welcome a healthy, loving relationship.

I naturally attract perfect relationships into my life.

People that Bring Out the Worst in You

Fuck Letting People Bring Out the Worst in You

Have you ever looked at someone you know and felt disgusted? Have you ever been around someone and thought to yourself: *If you would change, I will be happy.* You ever hung out with a friend and when you left from him/her you felt relieved because he/she sucks the energy out of you with his/her negativity. Wakeup call! You control the way you feel at all times. Even if you can't help being around someone that is negative, you still control the way you feel. A person does not have to change the way they are in order for you to feel positive. If you think that your happiness relies on someone else fitting your image of how they should be, then you will never be happy. You don't have to choose to feel disgusted if you look at someone who you define as disgusting. Your energy doesn't have to be infected by someone who is negative.

It is powerless to react negatively because someone else is negative. You don't have to stoop down to the negative energy level. Stay up there. Stay positive and you will notice that people will either grow or go. Make them meet you where you are, don't go back to where they are. A good practice is to focus on a positive aspect in everyone that you deal with and in every situation that you are experiencing each and every moment. The only benefit of recognizing the negativity in others is to drive you to your power of choice.

Every moment is an opportunity for you to choose. You can either choose negativity or positivity. There is not an in-between. You have to make a choice and your choice will determine your future moments. You attract what you give. If you hate someone for being who they are, you will receive the hate you give. If you feel drained from being around someone, you will get more drainage. Be who you want to see. If you want to have more positive encounters with people, you have to be more positive. If you want to receive love and support from people, be more supportive. If you let people bring out worst in you then you are just as bad as they are. You want to see more positive people around you or in this world, focus on that. Do not focus on the negativity because it will create more negativity. Be the person you want to see. Act in ways you want to see others act.

Meditation: Healthy Relationships

I am attracting warm and helpful people into my life.
I choose to be a friendly person to everyone I meet.
Good people come into my life every day.
All my relationships are now meaningful and supportive.
I choose to give positivity and warmth in all of my relationships.

Every day I attract more and more positive people into my life.

People love being around me because I am positive and I love being around positive people.

I attract all the right people into my life.

I look forward to happy moments with the people I encounter.

I accept empowering relationships.

I am supportive and dependable.

Section 9
Letting Go of Negativity

"I learned, working with the negatives can make for better pictures."

– Drake

Negative Thoughts
Fuck Negative Thoughts

We have a million thoughts flowing through our heads daily. Most times, they are the same thoughts we thought yesterday, and the day before yesterday, and the day before yesterday, and the day before yesterday, and the day before yesterday. Well, you get it. We have the ability to stop what we are thinking and think different thoughts. We get to choose the thoughts that we think about, so why choose to think about the negative ones. Most times the reason people choose to think about the negative ones is because they are not really choosing. People are like robots. We have automatic responses without thinking. I challenge you to challenge the negative thoughts that pop up In your head by being mindful about what is going on in your mind. Ask yourself why you are thinking the negative thought? Every time you have a negative thought, think of an alternative thought about the topic that feels better. Be the observer of everything that is going on in that head of yours. It is very challenging. It takes practice. But in the end, it is worth it. Once you get a handle on your negative thinking, you get a handle on your life.

Can you pinpoint a repetitive thought that you always have almost daily?

What negative thoughts have you had today?

Can you think about 20 things that are positive?
Things you love, love to do, love to see, love to eat, love to have, things you like/appreciate/value…

Meditation: Releasing Negative Thoughts

If a thought or belief does not serve me, I let it go.

Today I am breaking out of old patterns and rewriting old programs in my mind.

I release all negative energy from my mind and body.

I quickly dissolve all negative thoughts that limit my potential.

I release all old ways of thinking and eagerly welcome new ones.

I happily let go of thoughts that pull me out of the present moment.

I easily relax and let go of all the negatives in my life.

I easily let go of all disempowering thoughts.

Making Choices with Negative Energy

Fuck Making Choices with Negative Energy

Anger, frustration, sadness, and so on, can lead to motivation. For example, you can be so frustrated with your situation that you come to the conclusion that you want a better situation. That's cool! Now you have the desire to be, do, or have better. But wait! Don't make moves when you are in the middle of a frustrating feeling. You can't get to a happy destination on an unhappy journey. You have to bring yourself to feeling good. Remember, you attract what you give out. I repeat, you receive what you give! If you are giving out feelings of frustration, you will get another situation that makes you frustrated. It can be a small frustration, like when you realize you didn't grab a towel when you are done with your shower. It can be a major frustration like your car breaking down on the expressway. If you give out frustration you will get more frustrating circumstances.

Even if you do get a better situation, you won't get the best situation unless you are feeling your best.

Let's say, you are working at a job that you dislike. The feeling of displeasure is negative. You quit and search for a new one. If you are carrying feelings of negativity when you are searching for a new job, you will get a new job and it's going to be something about it that makes you feel displeased. It may be a bit better, but it won't be fulfilling. Same thing with a significant other. You ever realize someone will keep saying, "Why do I keep attracting the same people?" Because they are focused on what they don't like about the person they are with. Did you leave your last relationship out of frustration? Or did you leave out of the satisfaction of knowing your worth? Are you aware of the angle you are coming from? The message that you tell yourself is important. You can either roll with messages like: I am never getting a person like him anymore. She did me so wrong. I'm tired of feeling like there is something wrong with me. All men are the same. OR you can rock with messages like: I am deserving of a perfect relationship, the next relationship I get will be the best relationship ever, I saw a couple the other day and they looked so in love, I am only going to settle for what I deserve, and I deserve the best.

You don't know what angle a person is coming from until you see the results in their lives. You can think you have someone figured out, but you don't have to try. The proof is in the living. So like I said, don't make moves when you are feeling negative because the thing that comes out of that will be negative. Think about a student that failed a test that he has to pass in order to graduate. He has one more opportunity to take it again. He can use that negative experience of failing and allow it to bring him down. He can

102

study for the upcoming test in worry, fear, anxiety. Studying like that will fog his mind. It will make it so hard to concentrate if he is thinking about his past failure and if he is worried about failing again. That negative energy will suck the energy out of him and he won't feel like studying. The alternative feeling is a feeling of positivity. He can tell himself things like, *I have another chance at success, I can pass this test like my colleagues, thank God I am able to take the test again. I am going to graduate.* He can meditate before he opens the books and notes so that he will have a clear mind and the information will stick. He can be so motivated to pass that he feels good about the upcoming test. He will use the failure as a motivator to do better the next time. That positive energy will fuel him and give he the boost to stay up late nights to study. It will motivate him to reach out to a tutor if he needs help. It is up to you to decide how you will be driven by a negative experience. Will you be driven in a negative or positive direction?

It's impossible to never feel negative. If you never feel negative that means you are dead. If you are living you will always come across things you don't like, things you want to change, things that may hurt, and things that are not desirable. Let the negative feelings drive you to be still, to meditate, or to pray. Out of those practices, you will get the best answer on what move to make and when to make it. It's okay to have a negative feeling because it can be an indicator that you want better. It can be a motivator for you to go get something different. With that being said it's not okay to keep a negative feeling. Use it to your advantage and then let those negative feelings go!

Who or what can trigger negative emotions within you? Why do you ALLOW him/her/it to affect you negatively?

What are some things that you can think about or do to make you feel better before you make decisions out of negative feelings?

Meditation: Making Choices

When at a crossroads, the right path will be revealed.

Following my intuition keeps me safe and sound.

I know my inner wisdom will guide me to the right decision.

I will be decisive when the right decision appears before me.

I have the ability to make wise decisions.

I tap into my spirituality to make decisions even if they are minor.

I choose to remain calm relaxed and clear-headed in every decision I have to make.

I completely trust myself to make positive choices.

I intend to live my life by choice, not chance.

I have faith that my decisions will benefit all areas of my life.

Section 10: Act with Purpose

"I'm not going to sit at your table and watch you eat, with nothing on my plate, and call myself a diner. Sitting at the table doesn't make you a diner."

– Malcolm X

Walk It Like You Talk It
Fuck Talking It, Walk It

People talk all day long about what they are going to do, but you don't see them do it. What they are going to change, but they asses still the same as they were a decade ago. Where they are going to go, but they been in the same place forever. Making the same New Year resolution year after year. Don't be that person that doesn't walk it like you talk it. Practice what you preach. But even better is don't preach. Just do it, you don't have to talk about it.

Everything doesn't have to be said. Everyone doesn't have to know everything you have going on. Your actions will speak for you. Plus, when you don't have your own business set in stone, you leave yourself open to opinions and commentary from others which may affect your energy and how you move. On top of that, if things don't pan out the way you want them to, you start feeling a negative way because you told X amount of people about your plan and now you think they are going to be thinking *what happened to you doing what you said?* Then that negative thought will create feelings that don't feel good. You may feel like you didn't live up to the expectations that you created in the first place. Just don't open yourself to that. When you move in silence, people don't know what to attack. When you move in silence, you won't open yourself up to people saying you can't do it. You won't get people asking you all types of questions you may not have the answer to yet, but they start making you second guess yourself because they are second-guessing your abilities.

A lot of accomplished people move in silence. They link up with those who are key players in making the desire happen and they make it happen. Most people who try to broadcast what they are doing are those who are trying to get some praise or validation from others. You don't need that! If you are looking for validations from others, you may want to pause on making any moves and get your belief system in line. A lot of people are not in the position to validate you because they are seeking validation for themselves. Yes, it feels good to have support. Most times other people are essential factors in executing your desire. So don't walk around thinking you never need anyone. In order for a business to be successful, it needs consumers. In order for a song to go platinum, it needs listeners. We all need support at some point. What we don't need is to tell everyone what we have going on for the sake of validation or for the sake of trying to feel motivated to do what we want to do. Your blessings aren't for everyone, so everyone won't get it. Everyone won't support it. Everyone won't be enthusiastic about it. If you get it, if you support it, and if you are enthusiastic about it, that is all that matters.

What do you keep saying you are going to do eventually?

When are you going to stop putting off that thing you always talked about?

Meditation: Be About It / Action

I accept that I don't need to know everything in order to make a start.

By taking positive actions, I bring more positive results into my life.

I now act like the person I dream of becoming.

I am dedicated to doing everything it takes to reach my highest potential.

I am ready to do whatever it takes to make my dream a reality.

I control my life with the positive actions I take.

I am putting my mind, emotions, and actions to work for what I want in my life.

I empower my dream by directing all my thoughts and actions toward manifestation.

I am determined to go further each day.

I am unstoppable.

I have all the necessary power to do all I want to do.

Doing Things You Don't Want to Do

Fuck Doing Things You Don't Want to Do

When you do something that you really don't want to do, you don't feel good. When you do something for someone else because you don't want to let him or her down but you really hate doing it, you let yourself down. When you do something for someone else because you feel like you will betray them if you don't, you are ultimately betraying yourself. Guess what: Self-betrayal is the worst betrayal.

You have the ability to use two simple letters when you really want to use them, the N and the O. NO! If someone asks you to do something and in your head you are huffing and puffing thinking, *this bitch always asking me for something. Or I don't have time to do this today, but I'm going to do it anyway so he won't be mad. Or I'm tired of going into my bank account for this broke ass.* I'm talking about those types of things. Stop it. Stop going against your feelings to satisfy someone else's feelings.

When it's all said and done, when you honor yourself, you are making the correct decision and everything else will fall into place.

Now you may be working a job that you don't like, and you may be telling yourself that you have no choice to do the job that you do not want to do. So now what? Okay, is that job the end all be all? While working that job, are you putting energy into your own business or what you really want to do? Are you actively seeking another job in your spare time? Are you thinking you are stuck for the rest of your entire life working that job that you don't like? You have to believe that if you are in a situation that doesn't feel good right now then it is temporary. You are the one who makes it permanent by giving up and giving in. Knowing that it's temporary will give you a whole new attitude about the job you dislike. You can go to work with a smile on your face thinking to yourself, *I won't be here soon, suckas!*

You can thank God for the blessing that you do have at this very moment to have a source to make money, eat, have a roof over your head, and clothes on your back. You can thank God for the blessing that you do have at this moment to have a source to get experience. You can thank God for the blessing that you do have at this moment, so the next moment will be blessed. When you change your negative perception to a positive one, things start getting better and you will be presented with opportunities that you don't have to complain about.

Revisit these questions every day:

What did you do today? Or what do you plan on doing today?

Is it necessary or important to do what you did or what you are going to do?

What small thing can you do today that will bring you a step further to your desire?

Meditation: Honor Thyself

I listen to my inner being and honor the voice of my soul.

I make my dreams my highest priority in life.

I choose what to do and when to do it.

I am in control of my time and what I spend that time on.

I choose to do those things which bring me the greatest satisfaction.

I know what is most important to me and I attend to these things before all else.

I reserve my energy for the important things in my life.

I simplify my life by concentrating on doing things that feel good to me.

Every moment that passes I am making sure I am doing exactly what I should be doing.

I take time to enjoy my life.

Section 11: Timing

"When we spend our time looking at what other people do or what they have, we deprive ourselves of the opportunity to see our own value."

– Les Brown

Counting Time
Fuck Counting Time

We put time limits on everything. Time will have you fucked up. Mainly because when living your life according to time, you are living your life according to when other people accomplished something. Or, you are living your life based on a timeline that society has set. If you don't hit certain goals by a certain time, FEAR creeps up on you. If you think you cannot be happy until you accomplish something specifically, then you won't be happy.

It is time to let go of time. Focus on what you want and why you want it and go for it. Don't judge the way you move. Don't judge the way you don't move. Go with what feels good. It's best to keep your eyes on the prize and not the clock. If someone asks you how you are progressing, simply respond with, "Everything is happening in God's perfect time." That way, you won't feel under pressure to live up to others' expectations.

Most times when people focus on time, they add more time to what they want. If you think about it, when you are focusing on not having something at a specific time, you are giving your energy to getting exactly the opposite of what you want. You are giving your attention to the fact that you don't have something or haven't accomplished something and that is counterproductive to cutting down the time it can take to manifest your desire. That is because more than likely, a negative feeling is associated with time. Sayings that have a negative connotation are: when is it going to happen for me? I've been doing this for so long, maybe this isn't for me. We have been trying for a long time and it hasn't happened. It takes a long time and hard work to accomplish that. It's taking me longer than other people. So again, it's best to let go of time talk and just focus on what actions are in your power to take. Most times when people give up, that is when things happen for them. Giving up is when people let go of resistance. They stop fighting for something which allowed what they were fighting for to flow into their lives. Let what you want to flow. Let go.

Have you been waiting for something to happen for you?

Did you take all the necessary steps in your power to accomplish what you want?

What else can you do that can keep you happy and distracted so you can get into a state of allowing?

Meditation: Patience

I do not have to wait for the perfect life because my life is perfect here and now.

My life unfolds at a perfect speed.

I exercise patience in all that I undertake.

I am free from yesterday and I am free from tomorrow.

I know that all great accomplishments require patience and persistence.

Having to wait is a perfect opportunity to be still and grow within.

What I want does not affect my patience.

Every moment of every day, I am becoming more and more patient.

I conquer impatience by finding more interesting things to do while I wait.

Unfinished Tasks
Fuck Unfinished Tasks

Many people have several talents and most successful people have their hands in multiple things. HOWEVER, you have to see things through to the finish line before starting something new or continue to the finish line while you are starting something new. Don't just stop doing the first thing. If you don't fully execute something and you are doing everything, you will find that you are spread thin, giving a little bit of energy to this and little bit of energy to that and neither this or that is being completed. A lot of talented people are talented in several areas. With that being said, a lot of talented people do not fully succeed in all areas and sometimes they do not fully succeed in any area because they aren't putting enough energy into any of them. "The jack of all trades, master of none" sort of speaking.

I was guilty of doing that. I would start writing one idea, come up with a new idea and then I'd start writing the new idea leaving the old one unfinished. Then I'd go back to the old one to write some more, leaving the new one unfinished. I had to sit back and realize that nothing was getting completely done. I'm not a they sayer, so I am not going to say that because this happened for me that it will happen that way for you. Some people are great at doing more than one thing at the same time. But this goes beyond just doing more than one thing at the same time. Many people can do more than one thing at the same time, but many people are not accomplishing several goals at the same time. If you find that you are spread thin, you have many hopes and dreams and none of them are accomplished, and if you have incomplete tasks that you want to complete, you have to change up how you prioritize. Go hard, go all in and get what you want done! Stop stopping then going, then stopping then going, then stopping and going. Okay, I'm stopping. You get the point.

What is something that you already started doing but stopped?

Do you plan on starting it again? Why or why not? Where are you going to start?

Meditation: Completion

I always do the right things at the right time.
I am making time in my life to do what I need to do to manifest my desires.
I do what needs to be done when it needs doing.
I easily resist the temptation to give up.
I have all the time I need to accomplish all that I want to do.
I have the power to complete everything I want to do today.
I identify my priorities and plan time to complete them.

I know that all time is precious and therefore spend my time pursuing my dream.

I know that I must make time for the things I want in life.

I know that the only time that matters is NOW.

Section 12
Physical Well-Being

"How far you go in life depends on your being tender with the young, compassionate with the aged, sympathetic with the striving, and tolerant of the weak and strong. Because someday in your life you will have been all of these."

– George Washington Carver

Fear of Aging
Fuck the Fear of Aging

I've seen 80-year-olds who were bedridden and mindless. But there are people like Ernestine Shepherd who is in the book of world records for being the oldest bodybuilder. At 80, she was getting out to walk and run ten miles in the morning. She works out in heels and she is in phenomenal shape. The type of older person you will be is up to you and the choice starts in your mind. It starts with your perception of aging.

Do you believe you have to get old and bent over with an aching back, arthritis hands, and a lost mind? Or do you believe that you can remain as strong as possible, sane in the brain, and active? Everyone doesn't age the same and a lot of the differences depend on the mentality of aging.

One of the biggest ways to age badly is to stress. Stress causes many illnesses. It causes body aches and digestive issues. It takes a toll on how you physically look. It causes red eyes, black circles under your eyes, and hair loss. So, try your best not to stress and try your best not to stress over aging because you can't stop it. Stressing will speed it up. You're going to age, so why not do it peacefully, gracefully, and acceptingly.

Are you afraid to get old? Why or why not?

Do you think you are going to suffer when you get older?

Why do you think there are differences in the way people age?

Meditation: Youthfulness

I was born of the spirit and I continue to live in the spirit.

Every cell in my body vibrates with eternal youth.

The cells of my skin continue to regenerate and renew.

I know that I am only as old as I think and feel.

Every day my body is filled with incredible youth and vitality.

Every day I am more youthful and full of life than the day before.

I have the energy and enthusiasm of a child.

I intend to remain youthful and vibrant every day of my life.

I maintain a youthful appearance by constantly thinking positive thoughts.

Every day my body is filled with incredible youth and vitality.

My belief in my soul's eternity is reflected in how I look and feel.

Illnesses and Disease

Fuck Illnesses and Disease

We are physically affected by our feelings. When we worry, stress, or get depressed, we put our immune systems in a vulnerable state. You don't even have to be worried about getting sick to get sick. All you have to do is worry about anything. When you're nervous, your stomach may get upset. When you're mad, your head may hurt or blood pressure can rise. Ever notice when a kid cries hysterically, his nose may start running. There is a mind-body connection to every single feeling you experience.

If you worry about illness or disease, you are bound to experience illness or disease. You may not attract every disease you think or worry about but you will attract something. Everything starts in the mind. I want you to do this exercise real quick. It takes a few seconds. Close your eyes and think of something that makes you sad, angry, or ready to cry. Something you would define as negative. It can be a loved one dying, a tough breakup, Donald Trump tends to ruffle some feathers. If he ruffles yours, picture him. Now as you hold whatever negative thought in your head, I want you to actually feel the thought in your body. Where does the thought travel in your body? Stomach?

Head? A throb in your throat? Follow the thought. After you sense where that thought is and experience the sensations, allow your mind to go blank. Next, I want you to think about something that is positive to you. Something that brings you joy and happiness. The birth of a child, getting some good loving, LeBron James having a potentially good team again to get another championship! That's mine as I currently write this. Anything positive to you. Now as you close your eyes and hold that thought. Follow that thought. Follow the feeling. Do you loosen up? Get butterflies? Face automatically smirks? Feel some tingles somewhere. Experience those sensations and note the differences in your body between negative thoughts and positive ones.

If you really give your attention to every thought you can sense every feeling you produce. Many people don't realize that their bodies are feeling bad when it is feeling bad. But every negative thought that you have, produces a negative vibration inside of you that causes you to feel negative. You can eliminate so many ailments by simply eliminating negativity in your life. By simply choosing to be positive, think positive, and speak positive.

If you are in the midst of experiencing a disease or illness, it's best that you release resistance. It's there already so, being mad about it isn't going to cure it. Complaining, crying, and talking about it won't cure it. You need to talk about the outcome you want. You should focus on what you want: to heal. Focus on being healthy. Anything other than good health should be disregarded. If someone asks you, how you are doing. It's okay to say that you are getting better day by day. Or you can say I'm doing good because

126

I put my health in God's hands. It's not a lie. You are speaking it into existence.

Do you believe everyone has to suffer at some point in life health-wise?

Do you believe your health will suffer at some point in your life? Do you believe you can get better if you are suffering?

Why do you hold the beliefs you have about health and disease?

Meditation: Health and Wellness

I willingly relinquish every thought that might impair my health.

As I take control of my mind, I take control of my body.

Day by day, I am getting better and better.

Divine love flows through every cell in my body.

I send love and gratitude to every part of my body.

Every fiber of my being is vital and vibrant.

I allow myself to be in good health at all times.

I am blessed with well-being and health.

The divine power has the ability to heal my body.

I know that abundant health and wellness are my natural birthright.

I plan to live long and healthy.
I thank my body for my continued well-being.

Section 13
Count Your Blessings

"No matter your situation, there is always something to be grateful for and that's how we make room for the blessings."

– Jada Pinkett-Smith

Gratefulness
Fuck Being Ungrateful

Count your blessings. Count your blessings. **Count your blessings**. There are some people that didn't wake up this morning, but you did. So that is one blessing that you can count. I used to get tired of hearing, "there are people in way worse situations than you," whenever I was down and out, but the truth is, that is the truth. Other people being in more fucked up situations shouldn't be the reason you count your blessings, getting more fucked up situations if you don't count your blessing should be the reason you count your blessings.

It all goes back to reaping what you sow. If you continue to beat yourself up, if you continue to feel saddened, depressed, angry, and upset over a situation, you will dig yourself deeper and you will get more reasons to feel that way. On the other end, if you hold feelings of gratitude, you will get more things to be grateful for. Think about having a child. What if you took a child to six flags and they didn't say thank you? You gone redirect them to be kind and thankful for what you have done. You would be offended if they said, no I don't want to say thank you, I'm too busy thinking about all the kids that went to Disney World instead of six flags. You're not going to say, I apologize, let's go to Disney World. You'll most likely say fuck taking you to Disney World and I won't take you anywhere else since you are going to have that attitude. It's the same thing with you. How can one bless an ungrateful, crying, complaining, bitter, negative person? Side note: don't actually talk to the kids like that. Be gentle, loving, and kind. Teach them how to be grateful human beings. Teach them to be the people you want to see in this world.

Nobody expects you to walk around on a cloud and be happy go lucky 24-7… That's unrealistic. There will be situations that will bring feelings of despair and disappointment. But those feeling don't have to take over your entire existence. If you have a loved one that died. It's going to sting. It's going to feel like your world is over. But your world isn't over and if you have any other loved ones living, it's best that you don't dig yourself into a hole over the deceased one because it's going to have a negative impact on your loved ones that is still living. You have to work through those dark feelings and find a bright side. If someone pisses you off in the morning, you don't have to carry that anger around with you all day long, taking it out on people that had nothing to do with that specific situation. You know how you can have a banana or apple and there is a brown spot on a piece of it. You cut off the brown spot and eat the rest of the fruit. That is what you need to learn how to do in life. Cut out the dark spots and eat up the bright stuff.

It may be harder for some people to make themselves better in the middle of a slump. The key is to not think about it. Thinking about something is a choice. You can keep changing the topic of your thought every time a thought comes into your mind. You do have that type of power. You just have to use it. I'm sure there is one thing that you can think about to be grateful for when you are in the midst of tearing yourself down. If you have to get out and do something, get out, and do something. When it's all said and done, your gratitude does impact your life. Be more grateful.

How would you respond to a child that was ungrateful for something you provided? What makes you different from that child?

List 20 things for which you are grateful:

1.	**2.**
3.	**4.**
5.	**6.**
7.	**8.**
9.	**10.**
11.	**12.**
13.	**14.**
15.	**16.**
17.	**18.**
19.	**20.**

Meditation: Gratefulness

Every day, I give thanks for all that I have in my life.

Every day, I am becoming more and more grateful for what I have in my life.

Being grateful for what I have, brings more abundance into my life.

I welcome and appreciate the good things life has to offer.

The more I give thanks, the more things I have to be thankful for.

I sincerely appreciate the people, places, and events in my life.

I am thankful for the love and companionship.

I cherish each and every moment in my life.

I am so grateful to be alive.

Thank you, God, for loving and blessing me.

Complaining
Fuck Complaining

I was ten years old running and playing at my house. Lo and behold, I ran in the wrong spot (or what I thought to be the wrong spot at the moment) and a toothpick went up my foot.

I cried, screamed, and complained like I was losing my entire life as my grandfather tried to get the toothpick out of my foot. Finally, my grandfather aggressively yelled at me and told me to shut up. I looked at him in shock. "Why are you telling me to shut up and I have a toothpick stuck up my foot?"

"Crazy, old man!" I didn't say that out loud, but I surely had bad words for him flowing in my head.

Those bad words subsided when he made his message very clear. He told me my tears were not getting the toothpick out of my foot. My screams were not getting the toothpick out of my foot. My complaining was not getting that damn toothpick out my foot. So, what the hell is the purpose of doing all of that? My foot was still hurting whether I cried or not. He was right.

The screaming, crying, and hollering was actually making things worse. I was getting a headache, my sister was crying because she saw me crying in pain, and I was

135

irritating the people that were around me trying to help, causing them to complain about me complaining. Quite frankly, it was pointless.

I learned a valuable lesson from that incident. Hence the reason I said I thought I ran in the wrong spot when the toothpick went up my foot. It was the right spot because I grew from that experience. I gained knowledge: no matter what I'm going through crying and complaining is not going to help. Crying and Complaining actually caused more crying and complaining.

EX out the Crying and Complaining options when looking for solutions to make things better. Zip it. Breath. Relax and you'll be able to make the right decisions, find the best solutions, and make changes to whatever it is that is not going right in your life.

Do you like to hear other people complain?

Is there something in life you feel is worth complaining over? If yes, what?

If you answered yes above, how can you approach that same thing without complaining?

Meditation: Acceptance

Day by day, I am learning to trust the flow of life.

I accept and release everything in my life that I cannot change.

I take full responsibility for making the most of my life.

I accept complete responsibility for my emotions.

I totally accept those things beyond my control.

I take full responsibility for making the most of my life.

I accept others as they are, without trying to change them.

I am in the process of accepting life without judgment or criticism.

I allow myself to reach my highest potential through acceptance.

I allow myself to learn from all the relationships I have allowed into.

Section 14
Feeling Like You Are Enough

"To be a great champion, you must believe you are the best. If you're not, pretend you are."

– **Muhammad Ali**

Being Rejected
Fuck Feeling Bad After Being
Rejected

You may get turned down for something that you really wanted. Then here comes that FEAR. You walk away fearing that you are not good enough. You walk away fearing that you'll never hear a "yes" after being told "no." You walking away fearing that the time may never come. Fuck that fear. It's okay that you got turned down. It may not feel like it at the moment, but if you have the belief that everything works out for your highest good. Then EVERYTHING, including denial, is for your benefit.

Maybe you got turned down because you would have hated working there. Maybe you got turned down because you needed to train some more to be the best you can be at your particular talent. Maybe you got turned down because there is someone better for you. Maybe you got turned down because there is somewhere better you should be. Who the fuck cares why you got turned down? Wait, you do, right? Well, stop. The answer is not in the turn down itself. The answer lies ahead. Soon you will look back and say ah-ha, it's a good thing that that didn't happen for me at that time.

In the meantime, walk away with your head held high knowing that what is in store is better than before.

Being turned down can make or break you and the choice is yours. Just recall the play-doh and bubble wrap inventors were turned down for their original ideas, but they prevailed. You too shall prevail when it's all said and done.

Why do you think some of the most accomplished people were turned down before? (Steven Spielberg, Steve Jobs, Oprah, etc.)

Have you ever been turned down for something? If yes, can you see a positive out of that turndown?

Meditation: Self-Approval

The only person I need approval from is God, and
God already approves of me.
I value all my talents and abilities.
The more I love myself, the more things seem to magically
fall into place in my life.
Day by day, minute by minute, I approve of myself.
What I create has universal value.
My feelings cannot be hurt.
I release the need to prove myself to others.
I walk tall and hold my head high.
My self-worth grows each and every day.
It is my greatest desire to live each and every day with
unlimited self-esteem.

Perfectionism

Fuck Perfectionism

The only thing that is perfect about life is that there is no such thing as perfect. There is perfection in imperfection. Can you name one person that is perfect? Can you define perfect? I guarantee if you can name one person that you think is perfect, there will be one person that thinks the person you think is perfect is not perfect. Perfection is subjective. Perfection is in the eye of the beholder. With that being said, the most important viewpoint on how perfect you are is in your own eyes.

If you love yourself no matter how many times you screw up, no matter how many changes you go through physically, no matter what anyone else says, you will see how perfect you are. You were made out of perfection. While going through life, your view may have gotten obstructed, but if you try to see yourself as God sees you every day, you will feel your perfectionism. Don't feel bad for thinking you are perfect either. A lot of people want to make you feel bad for feeling things like perfection and confidence because they don't feel that way about themselves. Other people who know their worth won't view your perfect perception of yourself in a negative way because they understand it as well.

It's time that you THINK you are the perfect being that you are, it's time that you FEEL like the perfect being that you are, and it's time to act like the perfect being that you are. When you do that, you will no longer think of perfectionism as you do now. You will know that despite your imperfection, you are perfect.

You'll be unapologetically you.

What is a perfect person? A person that is...

By what standards do you judge what perfection is?

Meditation: Releasing Perfectionism

I release my need to be perfect.

The universe loves me just as I am.

I perceive the world around me in the most positive way possible.

I know being myself is more than enough.

I know that I am good enough to have the life I want.

My positive perspective protects me from the stresses of life.

I am learning to love myself as I am. Faults and all.

I strive to see the extraordinary in the ordinary.

I know that I belong right here, right now.

I love and accept myself as I am right now.

I accept only positive, compassionate points of view.

Section 15: Know Your Worth

"If I waited to be invited in, I never would have stood out."

– Serena Williams

Settling

Fuck Settling

Any time you accept something and you have to say "but I guess," you need to stop because you are settling. Let me give you an example of the "but I guess" people.

In a restaurant: "it's cold, but I guess I'll eat it."

At the cleaners: "It's a spot right there, but I guess it's clean enough."

Friends going out: "I don't feel like it, but I guess I'll go for a few."

At work: "that's your job, but I guess I'll do it."

At the salon: "that's not what I wanted, but I guess I like it."

I can go on and on, but I guess you get the picture.

You don't guess. You know. You know that you don't like whatever the circumstance is but you are going to settle anyway. Stop doing that and honor yourself. If you keep settling for stuff you don't like, you are putting it out to the universe that you have a settling nature. Universe is going to be like, *she asked for a big house, but she settles. Let her settle in this little shack. He asked for a Tesla but he likes to settle, so let him settle in this train they both start a T.* Stop settling! Stop having a settling spirit! Speak up on how you really feel and what you really want unless you want to keep settling and not actually getting what you want.

It is okay to be satisfied. It is okay to get the desires of your heart. It is okay to want the best out of your time, your money, your job, your spouse, or any other circumstance in EVERY area of your life. Don't feel guilty about wanting things done the way you want them done.

I remember I took my teenage sister to get some wings and the wings were not made correctly. She didn't like them, but she said she would eat them anyway. She didn't want to take them back because she felt like she would be in the wrong for complaining. No, it's not complaining! It's speaking the truth. You don't have to curse someone out or scream at someone just because they messed something up. You politely and confidently speak your truth and no one can argue against that. The wings were not made correctly and that was the truth. If she was lying just to get a certificate or free food, then that would be in the wrong. But what is more wrong is to eat something unsatisfactory. That can cause stomach aches, food poisoning, diarrhea, or anything else negative related to eating because you can't bless your food and view it in a negative way at the same time. Anything you do out of a negative perspective will cause a negative reaction in some form.

Speak up for what you want and how you want it. Don't settle for less because you'll always get things that make you settle or make you feel worse in another type of way. Don't settle for a relationship because you feel like you won't find another, don't settle for friendship because you feel like it's too late to make new ones, don't settle for a career because you feel like you put in too much time at one job, don't settle for anything that makes you feel smaller than your worth.

Is there anything in your life that you are tolerating or settling for?

You may not want to do anything about your tolerations right now, but how can you resolve them?

Meditation: Getting What You Truly Want

I affirm my desires with crystal clear intent.
I affirm my desires with unwavering faith.
I am in total control of what I think and say about myself.
I expect fantastic things to happen to me every day.
I have faith that my desires are being attracted into my life.
I can achieve whatever I set my mind to and from this day on my mind is set on success.
The law of attraction is transforming my life.
It is okay for me to have everything I want.
Every day I move towards having everything I want.
I am attracting the things that I truly want and letting go of the things that are holding me back.

Embracing You

Everyone is not going to like you. Be okay with that. Think of yourself as an acquired taste. Everyone doesn't like sushi, yet sushi is very successful at restaurants. If two people tasted the same plate of spaghetti, one person may dislike it, but the other person may think it tastes like heaven. You are the spaghetti. Everyone is not going to like you.

People grow up differently, have different experiences, and have witnessed different things creating a taste that they are used to. You may not be everyone's taste. People's background determines how they relate to you. All you can do is be you and love you and the ones that are supposed to like you will and the ones that are not going to like you won't. So don't try to please everyone. So many people that you may consider wonderful is whack to someone else.

What matters most is how you like yourself. If you like/love yourself, you will attract more people that like/love you. If you dislike and don't have love for yourself, you will attract more people that dislike you and don't love you. It all goes back to reaping what you sow.

With that being said, you will not like everyone you run across either. But when you walk in love, it won't matter if you like someone or not. You will allow them to be them because you know what it truly means to "Be you," "Do you," and "Love you." It's okay for someone to think differently from you, it's okay for someone to look different than you, and it's okay for someone to act differently than you. Division comes when everyone wants everyone else to be just like them, but that will never happen. Then that is when hate kicks in, when people are not able to accept and celebrate differences. People hate others because others are different from them, or people hate themselves because it is hard for them to embrace their own differences.

Embrace yourself, embrace your differences, embrace your life, and let others do the same for themselves. When everyone can accomplish that, we will develop a sense of appreciation for others and a deep love for ourselves.

What do you love most about yourself?

What beauty do you see in someone that is different from you? It can be someone you know or don't know personally.

Meditation: Self-Love

I am wonderful.
I am very important.
I am worthwhile.
I am excellent.
I am beautiful.
I am blessed.

I am loving who I am.

I am accepting of who I am.

I am important.

I am smart.

I am valuable.

I am special.

I am a child of the Most High.

Wrap-Up

In a nutshell, you will get what you fear, so fuck fear. Fuck getting the very thing you are afraid of getting. Do what is in your power to create the life you want to live. Live in faith and dwell in love to start attracting, manifesting, and creating the life you deserve. As suggested, you should go back and focus on one meditation at a time for at least 21 days to create the habit and program your mind to believe what you are affirming. If you need this to help you keep up with your progress, you can put a checkmark in each day for each meditation. It only takes five minutes out of your busy day to do this exercise.

You are worth those five minutes! The meditations can be found here: vimeo.com/angelmarie

Meditation: Fearless.

1.	2.	3.	4.	5.	6.	7.
8.	9.	10.	11.	12.	13.	14.
15.	16.	17.	18.	19.	20.	21.

Meditation: Money.

1.	2.	3.	4.	5.	6.	7.
8.	9.	10.	11.	12.	13.	14.
15.	16.	17.	18.	19.	20.	21.

Meditation: Abundance.

1.	2.	3.	4.	5.	6.	7.
8.	9.	10.	11.	12.	13.	14.
15.	16.	17.	18.	19.	20.	21.

Meditation: Releasing the Past.

1.	2.	3.	4.	5.	6.	7.
8.	9.	10.	11.	12.	13.	14.
15.	16.	17.	18.	19.	20.	21.

Meditation: Forgiveness.

1.	2.	3.	4.	5.	6.	7.
8.	9.	10.	11.	12.	13.	14.
15.	16.	17.	18.	19.	20.	21.

Meditation: Releasing Doubt.

1.	2.	3.	4.	5.	6.	7.
8.	9.	10.	11.	12.	13.	14.
15.	16.	17.	18.	19.	20.	21.

Meditation: Feeling Good Enough to Have Good.

1.	2.	3.	4.	5.	6.	7.
8.	9.	10.	11.	12.	13.	14.
15.	16.	17.	18.	19.	20.	21.

Meditation: Courage to Do What Others Can't Do.

1.	2.	3.	4.	5.	6.	7.
8.	9.	10.	11.	12.	13.	14.
15.	16.	17.	18.	19.	20.	21.

Meditation: Knowledge.

1.	2.	3.	4.	5.	6.	7.
8.	9.	10.	11.	12.	13.	14.
15.	16.	17.	18.	19.	20.	21.

Meditation: Self-Empowerment.

1.	2.	3.	4.	5.	6.	7.
8.	9.	10.	11.	12.	13.	14.
15.	16.	17.	18.	19.	20.	21.

Meditation: Choosing Your Own Reality.

1.	2.	3.	4.	5.	6.	7.
8.	9.	10.	11.	12.	13.	14.
15.	16.	17.	18.	19.	20.	21.

Meditation: Purpose.

1.	2.	3.	4.	5.	6.	7.
8.	9.	10.	11.	12.	13.	14.
15.	16.	17.	18.	19.	20.	21.

Meditation: Self-Acceptance.

1.	2.	3.	4.	5.	6.	7.
8.	9.	10.	11.	12.	13.	14.
15.	16.	17.	18.	19.	20.	21.

Meditation: Healthy Love Life.

1.	2.	3.	4.	5.	6.	7.
8.	9.	10.	11.	12.	13.	14.
15.	16.	17.	18.	19.	20.	21.

Meditation: Healthy Relationships.

1.	2.	3.	4.	5.	6.	7.
8.	9.	10.	11.	12.	13.	14.
15.	16.	17.	18.	19.	20.	21.

Meditation: Releasing Negative Thoughts.

1.	2.	3.	4.	5.	6.	7.
8.	9.	10.	11.	12.	13.	14.
15.	16.	17.	18.	19.	20.	21.

Meditation: Making Choices.

1.	2.	3.	4.	5.	6.	7.
8.	9.	10.	11.	12.	13.	14.
15.	16.	17.	18.	19.	20.	21.

Meditation: Be About It / Action.

1.	2.	3.	4.	5.	6.	7.
8.	9.	10.	11.	12.	13.	14.
15.	16.	17.	18.	19.	20.	21.

Meditation: Honor Thyself.

1.	2.	3.	4.	5.	6.	7.
8.	9.	10.	11.	12.	13.	14.
15.	16.	17.	18.	19.	20.	21.

Meditation: Patience.

1.	2.	3.	4.	5.	6.	7.
8.	9.	10.	11.	12.	13.	14.
15.	16.	17.	18.	19.	20.	21.

Meditation: Completion.

1.	2.	3.	4.	5.	6.	7.
8.	9.	10.	11.	12.	13.	14.
15.	16.	17.	18.	19.	20.	21.

Meditation: Youthfulness.

1.	2.	3.	4.	5.	6.	7.
8.	9.	10.	11.	12.	13.	14.
15.	16.	17.	18.	19.	20.	21.

Meditation: Health and Wellness.

1.	2.	3.	4.	5.	6.	7.
8.	9.	10.	11.	12.	13.	14.
15.	16.	17.	18.	19.	20.	21.

Meditation: Gratefulness.

1.	2.	3.	4.	5.	6.	7.
8.	9.	10.	11.	12.	13.	14.
15.	16.	17.	18.	19.	20.	21.

Meditation: Acceptance.

1.	2.	3.	4.	5.	6.	7.
8.	9.	10.	11.	12.	13.	14.
15.	16.	17.	18.	19.	20.	21.

Meditation: Self-Approval Releasing Perfectionism.

1.	2.	3.	4.	5.	6.	7.
8.	9.	10.	11.	12.	13.	14.
15.	16.	17.	18.	19.	20.	21.

Meditation: Getting What You Truly Want.

1.	2.	3.	4.	5.	6.	7.
8.	9.	10.	11.	12.	13.	14.
15.	16.	17.	18.	19.	20.	21.

Meditation: Self-Love.

1.	2.	3.	4.	5.	6.	7.
8.	9.	10.	11.	12.	13.	14.
15.	16.	17.	18.	19.	20.	21.

CPSIA information can be obtained
at www.ICGtesting.com
Printed in the USA
BVHW051214100821
614091BV00004B/289